Migración
Migration

Melvin & Gilda Berger

SCHOLASTIC INC.

New York Toronto London Auckland Sydney
Mexico City New Delhi Hong Kong Buenos Aires

Photographs: Cover: Randall B. Henne/DPA (Dembinsky Photo Associates);
p. 1: Mark Carwardine/Peter Arnold; p. 3: Mary Clay/DPA;
p. 4: B & C Alexander/Photo Researchers; p. 5: Scott Camazine/Photo Researchers;
p. 6: Randall B. Henne/DPA; p. 7: Bill Lea/DPA;
p. 8: Mark Carwardine/Peter Arnold; p. 9: Yves Lefevre/Peter Arnold;
p. 10: Tom & Pat Leeson/Photo Researchers; p. 11: Glenn Oliver/Visuals Unlimited;
p. 12: Fritz Polking/DPA; p. 13: Fritz Polking/DPA;
p. 14: Yva Momatiuk & John Eastcott/Photo Researchers; p. 15: Paul A. Souders/Corbis;
p. 16: Fritz Polking/DPA.

Photo Research: Sarah Longacre

ISBN 0-439-79176-6

12 11 10 9 8 7 6 5 4 3 2   6 7 8 9 10/0

Printed in the U.S.A.
First bilingual printing, November 2005

Muchos animales migran a lugares más cálidos en otoño.
Many animals migrate to warmer places in fall.

Los renos migran.
Reindeer migrate.

Migran en busca de alimento.
They migrate to find food.

Algunos pájaros migran.
Some birds migrate.

Migran en busca de nuevos hogares.
They migrate to find new homes.

Algunas ballenas migran.
Some whales migrate.

En otoño, muchas ballenas viajan a aguas más cálidas.

In fall, many whales travel to warmer waters.

Migran para tener sus crías.
They migrate to have babies.

Algunos peces migran a través del océano.

Some fish migrate across the ocean.

Algunos peces migran.
Some fish migrate.

Migran para poner huevos.
They migrate to lay eggs.

Algunos insectos migran.
Some insects migrate.

Migran en grupos grandes.
They migrate in large groups.

Algunas focas migran.
Some seals migrate.

Viajan miles de millas.
They migrate thousands of miles.

¡Nos vemos en primavera!
See you in the spring!